A WELL-SPENT LIFE

A WELL-SPENT LIFE

John W. Whitehead

TRI PRESS®
Charlottesville, VA

Thanks to
Rita Dunaway
Nisha Mohammed
Carol Whitehead
and
Mike and Patrice Masters

A Well-Spent Life.

For information, contact:
The Rutherford Institute
Post Office Box 7482
Charlottesville, VA 22906-7482

First published in the United States by TRI PRESS®

Cover design by Chris Combs

"Only a life lived for others
is worth living."
— Albert Einstein

TABLE OF CONTENTS

Chapter One
LOVING GOD

Pure and undefiled religion before God and the Father is this: to visit orphans and widows in their trouble, and to keep oneself unspotted from the world.

—James 1:27

What is your life about? If you're anything like the average church-going American, it might look something like this:

It's Monday morning. Your alarm sounds at 6:00 a.m. The first feeling you experience is one of dread. Is it already time to get up again? What happened to the weekend? More dread—a busy week is shaping up. Maybe you have a big project to finish by Wednesday, and you just can't seem to get it all pulled together. "Well," you tell yourself, "better get up and head to the office and get cracking." You shower quickly, grab some kind of supposedly healthy on-the-go breakfast bar marketed to busy people just like yourself, kiss your spouse and kids, if you have them, goodbye and rush off to work.

And it is work. Sure, there are occasional thrills and rushes that come along when you know you've done your job well. And that is totally valid. But aren't there times when you find yourself asking the question, "What is it all for?" According to the

Westminster Shorter Catechism, "Man's chief end is to glorify God and to enjoy Him forever."

But is this the purpose that your life reflects? How do you fit this into your 40- to 60-hour workweek? And if you're only "fitting it in," doesn't that reflect a life of misplaced priorities?

I believe every Christian wrestles with these questions. And while each person must personally untangle the details of this dilemma, I want to suggest what I am convinced is one component of the answer.

I submit to you that your life will only be imbued with meaning to the extent that you commit to investing it into caring for other people. This is not an original idea. It was Christ who said in Matthew 16:25, "For whoever desires to save his life will lose it, and whoever loses his life for My sake will find it." For Christians, this should be the final word. But the concept of giving of one's self is a component of virtually all religions. In fact, even non-religious people would say that caring for others is one of the highest moral imperatives.

Human beings are endowed with an innate sense that it is right and proper to give to others—particularly the poor, the outcast and the downtrodden. I believe this is because our Creator is deeply compassionate. The Bible is replete with entreaties and commands to care for widows and orphans. And the entire ministry of Christ is characterized by the compassion He showed to the poor, the sick and the dying.

Think about it for a minute—the entire Christian faith hinges on a truly amazing concept: the Creator of the universe becomes a baby, grows to be a man, becomes an itinerant preacher with little, if any, money or possessions and spends His time with prostitutes, thieves and poor fishermen. Thus the question: To what extent is your life characterized by a deep level of caring for those who are spiritually, financially, emotionally and physically needy? And now the more important question: To what extent do you actually show that you care for others by helping to meet their needs?

There is no doubt that the people who are the most like Christ are the ones who have committed their lives to improving the situation of others. They are people who have turned the energy of their lives outward, toward improving the lives of others. Rather than focusing on how they could achieve maximum comfort, power or prestige for themselves, they pour their lives into the betterment of those around them.

In fact, Christ conditioned the love of God on how we treat other human beings. When asked (by a lawyer) which commandment was the most important, He replied in Matthew 22:37-40:

> "You shall love the Lord your God with all your heart, with all your soul, and with all your mind." This is the first and great commandment. And the second is like it. "You shall

love your neighbor as yourself." On these two commandments hang all the Law and the Prophets.

Christ is clearly saying here that you can only love God by loving people.

Chapter Two
THE GOOD SAMARITAN

"So which of these three do you
think was neighbor to him who fell
among the thieves?" And he said,
"He who showed mercy on him."
Then Jesus said to him, "Go and do
likewise."

—Luke 10: 36-37

Most people are familiar in some way with the story of the "Good Samaritan." This parable contains the principle that, more than any other, has guided and motivated me in my life's work of defending those who cannot defend themselves. As you may recall, Christ told the time-honored story of this Samaritan man in order to explain how His followers should treat others.

The Samaritan in the story was on a journey when he came across a pitiful fellow who had been robbed, stripped, beaten and left for dead. Two religious men had also come upon him, but their response was to move to the other side of the road and proceed with their day's activities. However, when the Samaritan saw the poor man, Luke (Chapter 10) says that he "felt compassion" and bandaged the man's wounds. He then put the man on his own animal, brought him to an inn and cared for him. But not only that—his compassion carried him so far as to even leave extra money for the man with the innkeeper when he departed. He then tells the innkeeper that he will come back later to repay whatever the innkeeper must spend to care for the patient. Jesus ends His story by telling His followers to "Go and do likewise."

When I started The Rutherford Institute in 1982 with my family's entire savings of $200, my vision was to come to the aid of those who were persecuted and oppressed for their religious beliefs—the brave men, women and children who were willing to stand, and even suffer, for the freedoms we cherish. There is something inside me that simply has never allowed me to walk past people like Peter and Ruth Nobel, who were arrested for teaching their children at home; people like William Depner, who was arrested for engaging in pro-life protest activities; people like Nashala Hearn, who was suspended from school because she refused to violate her religious convictions by removing her Muslim head covering at school.

The Rutherford Institute exists to ensure that for people like these, the door to the courtroom is not hinged on the ability to pay for a lawyer. We exist to ensure that when a person's fundamental rights are violated, he or she will be able to turn to someone who genuinely cares about vindicating those rights; not just about the money-making potential of the case. So through a network of attorneys across the nation who volunteer their time, the Institute provides people like these with keys to the justice system. And we always provide our services free of charge. This is how we care for people.

Many times, litigation is not even necessary. Sometimes, all it takes to defend a person's civil liberties is an authoritative voice with the courage to say "enough is enough" and the legal training to articulate why. In such instances, The Rutherford Institute provides that voice.

Our staff puts together materials to inform the offending parties about why their conduct is unlawful, thus allowing them to make an educated decision about whether to persist in their chosen course of action. And although this costs us time and valuable resources, we are willing to pay the cost in the interest of preserving peace and allowing the offending party to preserve dignity.

Oftentimes, our clients' claims are based on government policies or regulations that run afoul of the First Amendment in some way. In these instances, we go so far as to offer our substantial expertise in assisting the government entity in rewriting the policy or regulation to conform to the requirements of the law.

A couple of years ago, a security guard threatened to forcefully remove a pastor from the grounds of the Alamo when the guard noticed that the pastor was about to lead his church youth group in a quiet prayer. In response to a letter from the Institute, the Daughters of the Republic of Texas, who manage the Alamo grounds, brazenly insisted that prayer was forbidden at this venerated public memorial. But ultimately, thanks to the dogged determination of one of our affiliate attorneys in Texas, the state of Texas decided to implement regulations—drafted with our assistance—to clarify the right of citizens to pray on public grounds. Thus, we allowed them to avoid a costly lawsuit and the public outcry that would have accompanied it.

Sometimes, however, it is necessary to take a case to court in order to defend the fundamental freedoms of the individuals who contact us for help. And this is very expensive. The costs of each case are covered by faithful friends across the country who believe our religious freedoms must be protected, whatever the cost. In many cases, these donations, in conjunction with our expertise and the commitment of our affiliate attorneys, pay big dividends by resulting in important changes in the legal landscape of our nation.

That was the case when one of our affiliate attorneys in Denver, Colorado, won a decisive victory against telecommunications giant AT&T in a case that had dragged on for several years. When Albert Buonanno called us, he had lost his job because he was unwilling to give up his integrity. AT&T had fired him for refusing to sign a statement saying that he agreed to respect and value all differences among employees, including sexual orientation. Buonanno indicated to his AT&T employer that he did not discriminate against gays and would not do so. He simply wanted to live consistent to his religious beliefs as a Christian. Thus, he could not sign the statement. Whatever your opinion is about whether differences in sexual orientation should be "valued," I hope that you share my sense of outrage at the prospect of employers requiring their employees to sign their name to this type of declaration of moral beliefs.

Thanks to the generous support of donors who share our commitment to helping others and the willingness of a Rutherford affiliate attorney in Colorado to volunteer

his time and energy to the fight, Albert
Buonanno was able to stand up to the giant.
The federal district court of Colorado held
that AT&T had failed to reasonably
accommodate Buonanno's religious
beliefs—a ruling that sent a clear message
to corporate America: Don't bully the little
guys, because there's someone out there
who will fight for them.

If you know anything about me or The
Rutherford Institute, you're probably thinking, "Well, it's not surprising that he would
help somebody who thinks homosexuality is
wrong since he's one of those Christian
conservatives." It is true that I am a
Christian. It is also true that the Institute
regularly assists other Christians who face
opposition as they exercise or express their
beliefs. In fact, our biggest percentage of
cases fall into that category. But that is
because Christians, probably more so than
adherents of other religious groups, have
increasingly been confronted with opposition as they try to live out their religious

beliefs in public life.

What might surprise you is that The Rutherford Institute is just as committed to assisting those who do not share my personal faith and convictions when their basic rights are violated. This is the Good Samaritan principle in action.

Chapter Three
HELP THOSE NOT LIKE YOU

The early Christian church cut across all lines which divided men—Jew and Greek, Greek and barbarian, male and female; from Herod's foster brother to the slave; from the naturally proud Gentiles in Macedonia who sent material help to the naturally proud Jews who called all Gentiles dogs, and yet who could not keep the good news to themselves, but took it to the Gentiles in Antioch. The observable practical love in our days certainly should also without reservation cut across all such lines.

—Francis Schaeffer

Each year, The Rutherford Institute handles thousands of requests for legal assistance. If the person has suffered a violation of his or her fundamental rights or is threatened with such a violation, we help. It's that simple.

There are four principles that characterize our philosophy as we strive to be Good Samaritans; principles that I hope you, too, will adopt to guide your own decision-making about how to spend your life. One, help those who are not like you. Two, when the cause is right, help even if you think you cannot win. Three, help no matter how big the opponent. And finally, help when it hurts.

Help those who are not like you. Someone who is truly emulating the Good Samaritan is just as quick to care for those who are unlike him as those who share his religious beliefs, moral philosophies, political persuasion or skin color. In the parable, the man who had been beaten, robbed and left for dead was a Jew. For a number of historical reasons, Jews and Samaritans were bitter enemies. And this is what makes the story truly remarkable. It's only natural that a person would help her friend when she is in need. But if you want to raise some eyebrows, care for someone who hates you. Better still, care for someone whom the world hates. Love the unlovable. Jesus said in Matthew 5:46, "For if you love those who love you, what reward have you? Do not even the tax collectors do the same?"

Most people are satisfied following the Good Samaritan principle as long as it only requires that they help others who are like them in some way. But, as I have just explained, these people have missed the essence of the principle. As a Christian, I regret to say that many people who would identify themselves as "conservative Christians" fall into this category.

For example, I received a letter from a woman who was irate because The Rutherford Institute was representing Nashala Hearn, a young Muslim girl who was suspended from school because she refused to violate her religious beliefs by removing her head covering. The lady who wrote to me had been a donor to our organization, but explained that she could no longer support our work if we chose to take this type of case.

This woman has missed the point of being a Christian! And so have any other "conservative Christian" organizations that would have helped out if it had been a cross that Nashala had refused to remove. My response to the woman's letter explained my reasons for helping young Nashala. Among them, I explained, was my hope that someday Nashala would ask herself the same question: Why would a Christian organization like The Rutherford Institute help a Muslim girl? And I explained my hope that as Nashala pondered this question, she would see that there are Christians who consistently practice their faith.

How unlike Christ we Christians are when we are willing to turn a deaf ear to those who need our help because they aren't like us. This is the very attitude of the religious men in the story of the Good Samaritan who crossed to the other side of the road, rather than help the man who was in need.

How quick we are to forget that Christ's harshest criticisms were for the Pharisees and Sadducees—the most "religious" people of His time. He did not turn in disgust from those whom we would consider the most despicable sinners around—prostitutes, thieves and the like. He simply saw them as lost people who knew they were sinners and treated them with tender compassion, gently pointing them to the Truth.

But the religious leaders of the day were a different story altogether. They were so caught up in being religious, in being sure to follow the letter of the law down to the tiniest detail, that they completely missed the substance of the heart of God—love and compassion for lost and dying people.

Chapter Four
HELP WHEN
YOU CANNOT WIN

We then who are strong ought to
bear with the scruples of the weak,
and not to please ourselves.
                    —The Apostle Paul
                    Romans 15:1

When the cause is right, help even if you think you cannot win. This is a tough one for attorneys like me to swallow because attorneys hate to lose! But with certain cases, the principle is so important that it's worth fighting for even when the case law is stacked against you. A great example of this is the case of Benjamin Ratner.

When Ben was in the eighth grade, he was suspended from school for four months after taking a knife away from a suicidal friend. This friend had passed him a note saying she had brought a knife to school, hidden in her notebook, and was contemplating suicide. Ben persuaded her to give him the notebook containing the knife and then put the notebook in his locker for safe-keeping. He planned to take it home and ask his mother to speak to the girl's parents (who were friends of the family). However, Ben was immediately suspended for possession of a weapon when a fellow student informed school officials that Ben had the knife in his locker. The school officials acknowledged that Ben's actions were "noble" and "admirable" and admitted that he posed no threat to himself or others. They nonetheless clung to their zero tolerance policy against weapons, forcing Ben to pay a huge price for being a true friend.

We knew from the start that this case was an uphill battle. Courts are loath to get involved with school disciplinary matters, and there was little, if any, case law to provide a firm foundation for our position. But it was wrong for Ben to be suspended for saving his friend's life.

We took this case all the way to the Fourth Circuit Court of Appeals, and we lost. We even petitioned the United States Supreme Court to reverse the appeals court ruling, but it refused. It was excruciating for us to see the judicial system wash its hands of this miscarriage of justice. But I would take that case again because I want young people to know that there is someone out there who will fight the good fight for heroes like Ben Ratner who are victimized by a disciplinary system that is devoid of common sense and good judgment.

The Rutherford Institute has taken on a number of zero tolerance cases similar to this one because we believe that schools are wrong to blindly apply a one-size-fits-all approach to discipline. We believe that by "taking the easy way out" of making considered decisions in this manner, school officials teach kids to despise and fear authority. That is something we are not willing to stand by and let happen.

In your quest to love and care for others, there will be many occasions when you stop to ask yourself, "Why should I bother?" You will struggle with the feeling that you're wasting your time because the need is so great that it seems far beyond your ability to fulfill. But please help anyway. Do you really believe in the God that you claim to love and serve? Then be faithful to do what He has called you to do, and leave the outcome to Him. I believe these "impossible" situations present the greatest opportunities for us to glorify God because when these overwhelming needs are met, the people around us will see that only God could have provided for them so thoroughly. Christ said in Matthew 5:16, "Let your light so shine before men, that they may see your good works and glorify your Father in heaven." Remember that the chief aim of our efforts, as we strive to help others, is to consistently live our faith and thus reflect Christ in our daily lives.

Chapter Five
HELP NO MATTER THE SIZE OF THE OPPONENT

And all the men of Israel, when they saw the man, fled from him and were dreadfully afraid.... Then David said to Saul, "Let no man's heart fail because of him; your servant will go and fight with this Philistine."

—I Samuel 17: 24, 32

The third key to implementing the Good Samaritan principle is to help no matter how big or daunting the opponent. This conviction was what led me to take up the battle of a petite woman named Paula Jones against the President of the United States.

Contrary to popular belief, I did not take the case because I hated Bill Clinton or because I wanted to sling mud at the Democratic Party. I did not take the case because I wanted to be famous. I took the case because Paula needed help and I believed that Bill Clinton had sexually harassed her. I absolutely believed that justice should not be swept under the rug simply because Clinton was the President.

In fact, the very name of The Rutherford Institute reflects the philosophy of Samuel Rutherford, a 17th-century Scottish theologian who maintained that no one, not even the King (or in this case, the President), was above the law.

Because most of our cases involve the First Amendment or other constitutional rights, the opposing party is often not a single face with a name but something much more nebulous: a government agency or entity. And anytime you sue the government, you face an opponent with seemingly limitless funds. But the size, position or complexity of your opponent cannot be a deterrent if you have purposed, as I have, to stand for those who have been wronged.

My experience has been that much of this persecution or oppression occurs at the state and local levels. Take the Hines family, for instance. Wally and Debby Hines lived out one of a parent's greatest fears when the government tried to take their two-year-old son from them! Far from child abusers, Wally and Debby are doting, loving parents. Their son, Wyatt, had been diagnosed with a rare bone disorder known as brittle bone disease. Their local Department of Social Services refused to believe that the boy actually suffered from the condition, however, and claimed custody of Wyatt after finding out about his recurring broken bones.

The couple was forced to flee overseas in order to keep their family together.

After extensive negotiations on their behalf, we arranged for them to return to the United States. But even then, the Hineses were forced to live under the supervision of a foster family for several months. The Rutherford Institute continued to fight for this family, helping them maneuver all the procedural landmines involved in this type of case until a judge ultimately dismissed all abuse charges against the couple.

As a father of five, I can assure you that I cannot imagine a more gut-wrenching experience than to be falsely accused of abusing your own child. And I regret to say that the breadth of authority that agencies like the Department of Social Services have is frightening. Moreover, challenging the actions of an administrative agency is an enormous task. To do it right requires lots of research, and lots of persistence.

However, if people like the Hineses are to have any hope of protecting their families from unwarranted governmental intrusion, there must be someone to whom they can turn for help—someone who will stand in the gap for them. We cannot be intimidated by difficult opponents.

In my experience, our nation's military is one of the most difficult opponents. Nonetheless, The Rutherford Institute has taken on numerous cases against them. For example, take the case of Technical Sergeant Jason Adkins. Sgt. Adkins, a fine Christian man, came under siege for speaking out about the military's forced anthrax immunization program.

The 32-year-old flight engineer had an outstanding career. In May of 2003, Sgt. Adkins was on the first C-5 flown into Baghdad during the Iraq War. And Adkins and his crew were recommended for one of the nation's highest awards of bravery—the Distinguished Flying Cross—for rescuing a crippled C-5 the size of a football field out of Baghdad with only three functioning engines.

But in October of 2004, Sgt. Adkins suffered the worst in a recent string of incapacitating migraine headaches, body aches and a racing heartbeat. An avid power lifter, he once weighed 252 pounds and could bench press 425 pounds before receiving his first anthrax vaccination. But by 2004 Sgt. Adkins' weight had dropped to 200 pounds and he struggled to bench press his own weight. Because of this, Sgt. Adkins went to see a flight surgeon. He spoke candidly with the medical staff about his recurring symptoms and the migraines—a flag word that translates into a disqualifying medical condition for any aviator. It is also a buzzword for Air Force personnel suffering some sort of harmful reaction to the anthrax vaccination. But Sgt. Adkins was accused of lying to get out of duty and was immediately issued a letter of reprimand so severe that Air Force lawyers claim it could potentially kill his military career on the spot. He also underwent humiliating public punishment by his superiors and peers, which was obviously intended to make an example out of him.

With the help of The Rutherford Institute, Sgt. Adkins filed a federal lawsuit in his ongoing fight for his constitutional right—and that of fellow suffering soldiers—to protected speech on matters of public concern. For us, being a Good Samaritan to Jason Adkins means being prepared and willing to take on the Pentagon.

Chapter Six
HELP WHEN IT HURTS

I am afraid the only safe rule is to give more than we can spare. In other words, if our expenditure on comforts, luxuries, amusements, etc., is up to the standard common among those with the same income as our own, we are probably giving away too little. If our charities do not at all pinch or hamper us, I should say they are too small. There ought to be things we should like to do and cannot do because our charitable expenditure excludes them.
—C.S. Lewis

As C.S. Lewis noted, in many ways, giving is the essence of love. In other words, giving that is not sacrificial is not true giving. But giving is not limited to money or material items. It means showing compassion on our fellow human beings. It also includes giving time to others, opening one's home and the general giving of oneself to serve others' needs.

I once had the privilege of working with a Christian theologian who was a tireless giver. In the last year of his life, this man was riddled with cancer. However, it did not cause him to forsake his work or keep him from one of his more tiring tasks—lecturing. Sometimes he would have to stop and sit down for a few minutes, but then he would rise and finish the lecture. And although it was very tiring and painful, he would often remain for hours after his speech to answer questions and discuss people's problems. This man, Francis Schaeffer, continued this until his death. A similar spirit must prevail in all believers if God is to be reflected in their lives.

True compassion must start with assisting those who need help the most. For example, why aren't more believers assisting the homeless? Why aren't more believers visiting nursing homes? Why aren't more Christians battling for the rights and lives of the unborn, infirm and aged? Christians should know that helping with physical needs is a condition precedent to meeting spiritual needs. Indeed, as the Apostle Paul admonishes in Romans 15:1: "We who are strong ought to bear with the failings of the weak and not to please ourselves." Jesus Christ reminds us that what we do to the least of these, we do to Him.

In one of my travels, I met a Christian man who worked as a barber in his spare time to meet living expenses. The major amount of his time was spent working without pay at a halfway house for AIDS victims, most of whom were homosexuals. The man said that when he first sought out what he saw as a ministry opportunity, he was told that Christians were not welcome because they were negative and lacked compassion. So he asked if he could simply wash dishes, which he was allowed to do. Eventually, through his caring and compassionate nature, he gained the trust of those around him and was able to minister to the sick and dying.

This is what true compassion is all about. It has nothing to do with weeping at tragedy, which might be more indicative of sentimentalism. Compassion is bringing justice and mercy to real-life situations.

Thus, if you want to be a Good Samaritan, you must choose to help even when it hurts. Meaningful help usually comes at a cost to the person who gives it. For The Rutherford Institute, the most obvious cost is financial. Although our affiliate attorneys handle our cases on a *pro bono* basis, the Institute pays all the expenses involved in bringing each case to an equitable resolution.

Given the number of cases we handle

every year, the amount of phone calls and e-mails we receive and the number and quality of educational programs and resources we produce, most people assume that our office is a massive complex staffed by hundreds of well-paid executives. But the truth is that we rent a small office building and employ a handful of people. So you can imagine how hard we all work. And by keeping a small staff in a modest office, we manage to keep our budget lean. In the end, this means that we can help more people. And although every single person on my staff deserves to be paid better and would be making more doing the same job at a private firm, they are willing to live on less because they believe in our cause.

But we could not continue to fight the good fight without the faithful friends who remember us in their prayers and financially support our work. The thousands of people whose hard-earned dollars keep the lights on at our office have considered the cost and determined that the eternal, intangible rewards they reap from their investment are worth it. They believe what Jesus said about treasure—that moths and rust destroy treasure stored here on earth. Thieves can break in and steal it. But those who store up treasures in heaven will have them for eternity. Tragically, though, many Christians become trapped in a lifestyle that leaves them little time or money to invest toward eternal treasures.

Chapter Seven
THAT WHICH
IS ESSENTIAL

The Spirit of the Lord is upon Me,
Because He has anointed Me to
preach the gospel to the poor. He
has sent Me to heal the brokenheart-
ed, To preach deliverance to the cap-
tives And recovery of sight to the
blind, To set at liberty those who are
oppressed, To preach the acceptable
year of the Lord.

—Jesus Christ
Luke 4:18-19

Like every other American, Christians face the almost irresistible temptation to spend their lives collecting temporal treasures. This seems to be an equal opportunity temptation—it strikes those at all income levels, all faiths, all races and all genders. It seems that we all want wonderful toys—the outrageously expensive sports car, an ostentatious home, a charming beach cottage, designer clothes, luxury vacations, etc.

Don't get me wrong—there is nothing wrong with having these things. But it's easy to forget that these things are temporal. They are temporary. And the biggest problem with spending your life collecting these types of treasures is that by the time you get them, the best part of your life—never mind an outrageous amount of money—will have been spent. As Winston Churchill said, "We make a living by what we get, but we make a life by what we give."

I know you've heard the old cliché that "things won't make you happy." What I want you to realize is that unless you purposefully choose another direction for your life, you will spend it acquiring things and maintaining them. And in the process, you will become a slave to them. You won't be doing this because you truly believe that things will bring you happiness. You will be doing it because you didn't decide to do something else with your life.

The truth is that chasing junk is the default mode for 21st-century Americans. It is continually foisted upon us through the media and the advertising industry. The Reverend Martin Luther King, Jr. once said, "We are prone to judge success by the index of our salaries or the size of our automobiles, rather than by the quality of our service relationship to humanity."

I believe this tendency is almost an involuntary one. We know that we aren't supposed to judge success in terms of dollars and cents. However, the very fact that we have to remind ourselves of this is proof that money and tangible things are precisely the yardstick of success that most modern-day Americans are using.

I urge you to switch out of default mode and thoughtfully determine how you will measure success. If you say "happiness," then go a step further and ask yourself how you will achieve that happiness. I'm asking you to decide what you want your life to be about. If you don't, I guarantee that your life will be about the worldly things that we have just described—things that rust, fall apart and ultimately end up in a junk heap somewhere.

When questioning the value of acquiring the pleasurable things that this world has to offer, most people will immediately ask themselves, "What's wrong with having nice things?" or "What's wrong with being wealthy?" The answer is: nothing. But you're asking the wrong question.

As John Piper says in his book *Don't Waste Your Life* (2003), you're occupying yourself with the question of what is permissible rather than focusing on the more important issue of what is essential. He recounts his own personal search for meaning in life this way:

> Somehow, there had been wakened in me a passion for the essence and the main point of life. The ethical question "whether something is permissible" faded in relation to the question, "what is the main thing, the essential thing?" The thought of building a life around minimal morality or minimal significance—a life defined by the question, "What is permissible?"—felt almost disgusting to me. I didn't want a minimal life. I didn't want to live on the outskirts of reality. I wanted to understand the main thing about life and pursue it.

If you're sitting around focusing on all the reasons why it isn't morally bad for you to have lots of nice things, you're already headed down the path of wasting your life.

This is because you're thinking about what is morally permissible rather than asking yourself what it is that is essential to a well-spent life.

It is astounding to see how generous American Christians are toward certain political parties or candidates. Don't get me wrong. I think it is fine for Christians, whom Christ called the "salt of the earth," to be involved in our country's political processes. But are passing laws and electing or even being the next popular candidate more important than caring for human beings? The church as an institution, and the individuals who comprise it, must be willing to get down into the nitty-gritty of life and minister, as Christ did, to the needs of the masses.

In his "Letter from Birmingham Jail," Dr. Martin Luther King, Jr. wrote: "There was a time when the church was very powerful—in the time when the early Christians rejoiced at being deemed worthy to suffer for what they believed. In those days the church was not merely a thermometer that recorded the ideas and principles of popular opinion; it was a thermostat that transformed the mores of society. . . . But the judgment of God is upon the church [today] as never before. If today's church does not recapture the sacrificial spirit of the early church, it will lose its authenticity, forfeit the loyalty of millions, and be dismissed as an irrelevant social club with no meaning for the 20th century."

I'm afraid that many, if not most, of the un-churched in our society, and particularly young people, think of the church as "an irrelevant social club." This is a tragic trend that we must reverse if we truly desire to imitate Christ. As 1 John 3:17 says, "But whoever has this world's goods, and sees his brother in need, and shuts up his heart from him, how does the love of God abide in him?"

You are probably thinking, "I'm willing to pay the cost. I'm willing to fight uphill battles for anyone who needs it and I'll take on any opponent." But there's one last thing. You have to do it. And although it sounds simple, this is where many people with great intentions stall out. Big dreams are dashed to pieces on the shores of reality.

I urge you not to throw years away while you live under the delusion that you'll start to care for others "as soon as" you become partner, you're making triple digits, your house is paid off, ad infinitum... Don't fall for it!

Maybe you've heard this quote by Alfred D. Souza, a Catholic Bishop in India: "For a long time it had seemed to me that life was about to begin—real life. But there was always some obstacle in the way, something to be gotten through first, some unfinished business, time still to be served, a debt to be paid. Then life would begin. At last it dawned on me that these obstacles were my life." He's right. Your life is passing by now. Don't put off doing what is essential to a well-spent life.

I believe that we are each called to

speak for those who have no voice; to pro-
tect those in danger; to care for those in
need. The fact that you are breathing means
that you are in a position to do that. You can
help to right the wrongs that have been done
to others. People who do not look like you,
perhaps. Maybe even people you do not
like. But they are people who are in need.
And you will be faced with a choice. Will
you help them, or will you cross to the other
side of the road? There is no neutral position.

So the question is—what will you do?
Will you use your education, your status,
your money, your life to gratify your own
desires? Or will you find the joy that comes
through giving from the abundance that will
be at your disposal to meet the more basic
needs of those around you?

In John Piper's book *Don't Waste Your
Life*, he tells a story of two women, Ruby
Eliason and Laura Edwards. Ruby was over
80 when she became a missionary in
Cameroon, West Africa. Laura, a widow,

was a medical doctor who decided to live out her final days serving by Ruby's side. In April of 2000, the two were killed when the brakes of their car failed and the car went over a cliff. Piper writes, "Was that a tragedy? Two lives, driven by one great passion, namely, to be spent in unheralded service to the perishing poor for the glory of Jesus Christ—even two decades after most of their American counterparts had retired to throw away their lives on trifles. No, that is not a tragedy. That is a glory. These lives were not wasted. And these lives were not lost."

Piper continues, "I will tell you what a tragedy is. I will show you how to waste your life. Consider a story from the February 1998 edition of *Reader's Digest*, which tells about a couple who 'took early retirement from their jobs in the Northeast five years ago when he was 59 and she was 51. Now they live in Punta Gorda, Florida, where they cruise on their 30 foot trawler, play softball and collect shells.'"

"At first," Piper writes, "when I read it I thought it might be a joke. A spoof on the American Dream. But it wasn't. Tragically, this was the dream: Come to the end of your life—your one and only precious, God-given life—and let the last great work of your life, before you give an account to your Creator, be this: playing softball and collecting shells.... That is a tragedy. And people today are spending billions of dollars to persuade you to embrace that tragic dream. Over against that, I put my protest: Don't buy it. Don't waste your life."

You have been given much. That means you have much to offer others.

Don't waste it.

Choose how you will spend your life.

And choose wisely.